D0914064

CLASS IN AMERICA

CLASS AND
EDUCATION

BY DUCHESS HARRIS, JD, PHD
WITH A. W. BUCKEY

Essential Library

An Imprint of Abdo Publishing | abdopublishing.com

ABDOPUBLISHING.COM

Published by Abdo Publishing, a division of ABDO, PO Box 398166, Minneapolis, Minnesota 55439.
Copyright © 2019 by Abdo Consulting Group, Inc. International copyrights reserved in all countries.
No part of this book may be reproduced in any form without written permission from the publisher.
Essential Library™ is a trademark and logo of Abdo Publishing.

Printed in the United States of America, North Mankato, Minnesota
042018
092018

**THIS BOOK CONTAINS
RECYCLED MATERIALS**

Cover Photo: Shutterstock Images
Interior Photos: Shutterstock Images, 5, 49; Louise Wateridge/Sipa/AP Images, 8; iStockphoto, 11, 25; North Wind Picture Archives, 15; Thomas J. O'Halloran/U.S. News & World Report Magazine Photograph Collection, 22; Red Line Editorial, 28; Nate Guidry/Pittsburgh Post-Gazette/AP Images, 30–31; Scott Terrell/Skagit Valley Herald/AP Images, 33; Rogelio V. Solis/AP Images, 37, 50, 84; Morgan Lee/AP Images, 42–43; Trent Nelson/The Salt Lake Tribune/AP Images, 46; Andrew D. Brosig/Tyler Morning Telegraph/AP Images, 55; Kevin Kilhoffer/Times-Courier/AP Images, 56; John Blanding/The Boston Globe/Getty Images, 59; Alan Spearman/The Commercial Appeal/AP Images, 63; Dave Collins/AP Images, 65; David Zalubowski/AP Images, 66; Monkey Business Images/iStockphoto, 69; Kathryn Scott Osler/Denver Post/Getty Images, 74–75; Spencer Platt/Getty Images News/Getty Images, 76; People Images/iStockphoto, 79; Bebeto Matthews/AP Images, 82; Benny Marty/iStockphoto, 87; Ted S. Warren/AP Images, 89; Mel Evans/AP Images, 91; Susan Walsh/AP Images, 96

Editor: Rebecca Rowell
Series Designer: Becky Daum

LIBRARY OF CONGRESS CONTROL NUMBER: 2017961138

PUBLISHER'S CATALOGING-IN-PUBLICATION DATA

Names: Harris, Duchess, author. | Buckey, A. W., author.
Title: Class and education / by Duchess Harris and A. W. Buckey.
Description: Minneapolis, Minnesota : Abdo Publishing, 2019. | Series: Class in America | Includes
     online resources and index.
Identifiers: ISBN 9781532114052 (lib.bdg.) | ISBN 9781532153884 (ebook)
Subjects: LCSH: Education--Demographic aspects--Juvenile literature. | Government aid to
     education--Juvenile literature. | Educational sociology--Juvenile literature. | Children with
     social disabilities--Education--Juvenile literature. | Social classes--United States--History--
     Juvenile literature.
Classification: DDC 301.451--dc23

CONTENTS

PRE-K
FOR ALL

A round noon on a typical weekday in New York City, approximately 70,000 four-year-olds take a break from their busy schedules to have lunch.[1] At Bank Street Head Start in lower Manhattan, students wash their hands and practice helping set the table before eating. One February menu included beef and mushroom stroganoff with buttery noodles. Head Start programs are designed to serve children from low-income families and children with disabilities. All students at Bank Street Head Start come from families that meet federal poverty guidelines.

Several miles south, at the Brooklyn Explorers Academy, prekindergarteners, or preschoolers, might sit down to a

This young girl gets much more than fun from her Head Start program in New York, including education, health, and nutrition.

plate of turkey breast, baked potato, and banana. The school is committed to healthy eating. It partners with a local farm co-op to make fresh, locally sourced meals for all the kids. Every breakfast and lunch at the school is made from sustainably farmed foods served on plates and bowls made of sugarcane fiber. Brooklyn Explorers Academy is an expensive private school. Most parents pay more than $25,000 a year in tuition.[2] However, for 20 students who entered a citywide lottery open to all four-year-olds and won a spot, this year of prekindergarten (pre-K) is free.[3]

HISTORY OF PRE-K FOR ALL

A few years ago, pre-K programs, especially the full-day ones now offered in many New York City public schools, were much less common. Now, it is typical for four-year-olds to take part in public school programs filled with play and music as well as the hard work of getting ready to read, count, and work well with others.

These 70,000 lunching four-year-olds are part of a New York City program called Pre-K for All. Both Bank Street Head Start and Brooklyn Explorers Academy are part of the citywide program. Starting in 2014, New York City guaranteed a free spot at full-day pre-K to every child whose family filled out an application—as many as 73,000 children.[4] Not every child is required to go to pre-K, but every child has the opportunity to do so. This means the New York City public school system expanded itself by an entire grade level, adding thousands of teachers and classrooms in the process. The program began as a way to fight income inequality by giving every child a head start to succeed in school.

To find a pre-K spot, families submit a ranked list of school choices. Public and private schools participate in the program, but not every child is able to go to his or her first-choice school. Because of the city's pre-K program, some kids end up at private schools that might otherwise cost tens of thousands of dollars a year, while others go to public schools or centers for early childhood education. All Pre-K for All schools have to follow similar standards. The city is responsible for enforcing uniform health and safety rules and supervising the hiring of trained teachers. And the city sets guidelines for learning and growth.

EARLY EDUCATION AND ACCESS

Research shows that early childhood education can have a lifelong impact on a person. One famous study of children born into poverty showed that kids who went to preschool were

New York City mayor Bill de Blasio urged parents to sign up for Pre-K for All while visiting the Bishop Ford School Site Pre-K Center in Brooklyn in February 2016.

more likely to graduate from high school and earn high incomes than kids who did not. Research by the University of Chicago indicates that for low-income children in particular, entering school at age four instead of age five can give a large and lasting academic boost.

The Pre-K for All program has supporters and critics. Many families in suburban New York are excited about the program and hope it will spread across the state. But some wealthy New Yorkers, whose increased taxes helped pay for the rapid hiring of new teachers, were angry about the program and tried to keep it from happening. They did not want to pay additional taxes to fund public pre-K. Some other New Yorkers criticized Pre-K for All for allowing all New York four-year-olds to get a free pre-K spot, even children whose parents are wealthy and can already afford to pay for private schooling. These critics believe the money for public pre-K should go only to families in need of help, not families that can afford tuition and simply want a year of tuition-free private school. These critics point to the fact that schools can give admissions preference to existing students, so at some private schools, many Pre-K for All seats go to families that already pay tuition at the school. Meanwhile, some lower-income parents may not know about the program or may have trouble finding good pre-K programs near their homes. Some people

3-K FOR ALL

Inspired by the success of Pre-K for All, New York City mayor Bill de Blasio's next program aims to expand full-day public education to include three-year-olds. The goal is to have 3-K available for 60,000 three-year-olds by 2021. The mayor is asking for more than $700 million from New York State and the federal government to make the program happen.[5] The total cost of the program is estimated at more than $1 billion.[6] The 3-K for All program faces criticism from some people in state government who feel that statewide pre-K should take priority over expanding to 3-K in New York City. In addition, some nonprofit day cares and preschool centers worry that they will lose their teachers to New York City public schools, which often pay higher salaries and offer better benefits. Other critics say the 3-K program will pour too much money into early childhood education without doing anything to improve public schools for kindergarten through twelfth grade.

argue that Pre-K for All would be fairer if it were only for some low-income families instead of for all New Yorkers. The debate over Pre-K for All raises vital questions about the roles of wealth and access in US education.

WHAT CLASS IS

Under US law, all Americans have the same right to an opportunity to learn. However, some of these differences in educational opportunity, access to resources and information, and outcomes are due to differences in class.

Class is a complex term with many meanings. Most societies divide people into groups with different amounts of power and different ways of life. These hierarchies are called class systems. In the United States, class usually refers to socioeconomic class. The word *socioeconomic*, which refers to a combination of social and economic factors, reflects the idea that money and social status are related. Socioeconomic class, which is also known as socioeconomic status, is based mostly on money. It can also be based on social and educational factors. According to a 2016 study by the Pew Research Center, approximately 29 percent of Americans are in the lower-income range. They live in households making less than $41,641 a year. Fifty-one percent of Americans are in the middle-income range, making between $41,641 and $124,924 a year. The remaining approximately 20 percent of Americans are in the high-income range and make

more than $124,924 a year.[7] These numbers provide a good starting point for understanding the nature of socioeconomic class, but they do not give the whole story.

Differences in income and wealth lead to differences in culture and social status—the "socio" part of socioeconomic class. Money and wealth influence the type of jobs people work, where they live, what they buy and do for fun, how they raise their children, and how they spend their time. Class also helps predict the amount of power a person has in society. For example, with an average wealth of approximately $8 million per person, members of the US Congress tend to be much wealthier than regular Americans.[8]

These differences in lifestyle and power can stay with people throughout their lives, even when the amount of money they make changes. For example, a young woman might grow up in a middle-income household and feel used to the privileges and cultural customs of her family background, even if her first few jobs after college do not pay much money. On the other hand, a middle-aged man who grows up in a poor household and later earns a high salary may still identify with the community and experiences of his lower-income childhood.

CLASS AND EDUCATION

Socioeconomic class helps determine whether children will attend private or public school and the kind of experiences they may have in school. Class differences help predict a child's success in school and his or her ability to enroll in and finish college. A child's education affects career options and earning potential. Therefore, class differences in education have lifelong effects and carry over from generation to generation.

The American cultural ideal of equal opportunity for all, including the opportunity to learn, often clashes with the realities of class difference. This means education policy is a constant subject of debate. Today, some of the most important controversies in education are about private funding for public education, equal opportunity in the education system, and education as a tool of economic competition and success. Many of these debates have a very long history, reaching back to the origins of the American education system.

DISCUSSION STARTERS

- Do you think all children should start school at pre-K instead of kindergarten? Why or why not?

- Do you think New York City should offer free pre-K to all residents or only to residents who cannot afford private tuition? Why?

- What does the term *middle class* mean to you? Why do you think most Americans identify as middle class?

HISTORY OF
CLASS AND
EDUCATION

E ducation is the way people learn about the world. It is the knowledge and skills that prepare a person for life as an adult. Different cultures have different ways of thinking about what an education is, why it matters, and who should get one. In the United States, most modern ideas about class and education have their roots in the culture of its European colonizers.

In medieval European culture, education was for priests, monks, and people wealthy enough to pursue jobs that required reading. It was also typically limited to men and very small numbers of women. Many early European colonizers, such as the Puritans, valued education as a way of studying the Bible and

For centuries, college education was limited to men, such as at Prague University in the late Middle Ages.

NATIVE AMERICAN BOARDING SCHOOLS

For much of American history, the US government had a policy of trying to force Native Americans to adopt the language, habits, jobs, and social structure of white American culture. The founder of the first Native American boarding school was military officer Richard Pratt. He helped lead a movement to separate Native American children from their families and communities and raise them in boarding schools. Pratt said his educational goal was to "kill the Indian . . . save the man."[1] He thought "killing" all traces of Native American culture would turn Native American children into assimilated citizens. A few government-run Native American boarding schools with voluntary enrollment still exist today.

training ministers. As the United States grew and expanded, so did educational opportunities. However, certain residents had more educational opportunities than others.

THE COLONIAL ERA AND EARLY REPUBLIC

Around the time of the American Revolution (1775–1783), many thinkers and pro-democracy activists began to call for public education. In Massachusetts, which had public schools as early as the 1600s and required everyone to learn how to read, this era was a time of greater support for widespread education through the elementary or high school level.

The educational work of Thomas Jefferson helps show some of the changes in class and education during the early years of the United States. This American revolutionary, president, and university founder thought good public education was necessary for a democratic republic. He wanted children to have a general education, learning subjects such as zoology and ethics instead of focusing on only religious learning. Jefferson believed in teaching girls as well as boys, and by 1850, girls made up one-half of all students in public school.

Jefferson's vision of a well-educated republic had many limits. He believed children of all socioeconomic backgrounds should have some opportunity for an education, but he also proposed a system in which most students would have to pay school tuition. Under his plan, only a few very talented poor children could receive scholarships. Jefferson helped found and plan the University of Virginia, which opened in 1825. It was a public university but charged tuition. And he was a slaveholder who participated in denying education and independence to people who were enslaved.

During this period of American history, slavery was legal and common, and millions of blacks lived in bondage with no legal rights. Enslaved people were denied the opportunity to get an education because slaveholders were afraid the ability to read or do official business would help enslaved people rebel. Often, enslaved people who tried to educate themselves suffered violent punishment.

Through the early 1800s, school education was mostly organized by towns, churches, or small settler communities.

Groups of children attended when they could, and the school year was short. Teachers would move from town to town. They were often poorly paid and had to teach students of all ages at once.

PUBLIC EDUCATION IN THE 1800s AND EARLY 1900s

The early to mid-1800s saw new inventions in public education. The Lancasterian method became fashionable in American cities. Named for its founder, Joseph Lancaster, the method told teachers to give their lessons to the oldest or most advanced students, who then acted like teachers to younger children. Lancaster believed this was a thrifty and efficient way of teaching poor children. The strategy was not popular for long.

During this time, reformers such as Horace Mann and John Dewey started to push for free schooling for all children. Mann was an elected representative in Massachusetts who believed strongly in public education. He created a state board of education and began an educational journal to spread his ideas. Mann said, "Education . . . is a great equalizer of the conditions of men."[2] John Dewey was a philosopher who believed democracy thrived when students could think and inquire for themselves. In the mid-1800s, Massachusetts passed the first state law making school attendance required.

After the Civil War (1861–1865) ended and slavery was abolished, a wave of new schools, colleges, and universities for newly free African Americans were constructed. The process of rebuilding the South after slavery, known as Reconstruction, helped create the Southern public education system. In the second half of the 1800s, the United States saw huge waves of immigration, mainly from Europe, as well as an industrial revolution that created many new jobs for immigrant workers. Factories and other businesses, as well as some church and farm groups, pushed against laws that limited child labor and made children attend school. Some immigrants, such as those living in Chinese communities in California, were not allowed to get an education. But some businesses came to

BOOKER T. WASHINGTON AND AFRICAN AMERICAN EDUCATION

Booker T. Washington was an educator, writer, and speaker who worked to improve education for African Americans during the period after the American Civil War (1861–1865) known as Reconstruction. Washington was born into slavery in Virginia in 1856. He was freed after the war. Washington received his teacher training in Virginia. In 1881, he helped found Tuskegee Institute, a school devoted to educating and training black students for the workforce. Washington thought moral and intellectual education combined with economic power would help black people achieve status in society. Other black leaders criticized him, including W. E. B. DuBois. He thought Washington's focus on individual uplift instead of social change ignored the significance of antiblack discrimination and oppression in American society.

HISTORY OF THE IQ TEST

In the early 1900s, a psychologist and former football coach named Henry Goddard decided to translate a French intelligence test and apply it to the American school system. He wanted to look into the origins of what he called "feeble-mindedness."[3] The French test, the Binet and Simon Tests of Intellectual Capacity, evolved into what we now know as the IQ test. "IQ" is short for "intelligence quotient." The test was supposed to measure a person's natural intelligence. Goddard wanted to use the test to advance his dangerously prejudiced goals for society. He thought it was important to separate citizens by intelligence and keep people of very low intelligence from marrying and having children.

In 1911, Goddard convinced public schools to use the intelligence test. Sometimes, people used these tests to try to prove there were inborn differences between people of different races and different socioeconomic backgrounds, even though one person's score on an IQ test can change over time. IQ tests are still used today. Many people do not know they were once used to justify isolating people with low scores or to prove racist theories.

see public education as a way of training immigrants and other low-income people as workers. These companies thought school would teach children and teenagers the skills and routines that would suit them to their jobs.

In the early 1900s, using intelligence tests to try to predict whether students should go to college or to trade schools became a popular practice. These tests, which were often based on biased ideas, were meant to figure out the future class of students while they were still young.

POST–CIVIL WAR AND BEYOND

After Reconstruction, many white communities tried to overturn the political and social gains made by black people after slavery.

The 1896 Supreme Court case *Plessy v. Ferguson* made racial segregation legal. For decades afterward, Southern schools were strictly separated by race, with black schools getting less money and fewer resources and with black students suffering discrimination. The 1954 Supreme Court case *Brown v. Board of Education* made segregation illegal and ended a major class distinction in American education. However, many communities protested or resisted the law, and the current American school system still shows signs of racial segregation. During segregation, a large gap existed between the academic achievements of black students and white students. After segregation ended, that gap quickly got smaller, but some differences remained.

After World War II (1939–1945), the United States emerged as the world's most powerful country, and the federal government started to get more involved in public education. From the years after World War II until 1991, the United States was engaged in the Cold War, an intense competition for world power with the Soviet Union. The US government wanted to become more powerful than the Soviet Union in every way. This included in the military, scientific, and financial sectors. The US government also wanted to spread its cultural influence around the world and pushed for democracy over Communism, the system of government the Soviet Union followed. Part of the US government's plan was to urge students to achieve in school and become the next generation of scientists and inventors. This time of government investment was also a time of anti-government

protest and activism. Civil rights advocates and other activists objected to unequal funding and widespread discrimination in the public school system.

The second half of the 1900s helped open some closed doors in education. Formerly all-male elite colleges and universities such as Harvard, Princeton, and Yale started admitting women as students for the first time. In 1972, the Title IX statute made sure that federally funded programs, including those at public schools, allocated equal amounts of money for men and women. Girls and women had been represented in schools for a long time. With Title IX, they started to gain more power and equality in the classroom.

DISCUSSION STARTERS

- Compare and contrast the role of education in colonial communities with the role of education in your community. How are they similar? How are they different?

- Why do you think many children in the industrial era worked instead of going to school? What were the benefits and drawbacks of choosing work over school?

- Joseph Lancaster thought children should be able to act as each other's teachers, rotating responsibilities as needed. Do you agree that children can be effective teachers? Explain your answer.

THREE

STRUCTURES OF
CLASS AND
EDUCATION

The history of class and education in the United States shows that class is about more than money and that public education has not always meant education for all. In many ways, the American class system and the American education system have been designed to give more opportunities to some people based on their race, gender, language, and physical and intellectual abilities. These differences in opportunity are some of the structural factors of class and education. They are "structural" because they are part of how these large systems have been built and part of how they function today.

Diverse classrooms allow opportunities for students from different backgrounds to learn more than the subjects they study.

Class shapes each person's life experiences and mind-set. People of different socioeconomic classes have different attitudes toward and experiences in the education system. These differences are key to understanding how class and education interact with each other.

RACE

Because of the way economic opportunities, living conditions, and social structures have been determined by race, separating class and race completely is impossible. In the United States, large gaps exist between the average incomes and resources of people of different races. For example, the median African American household has approximately 6 percent of the wealth—which is the total amount of money, investments, and valuable possessions—of the median white household. The median Latino household has approximately 8 percent of the wealth of the median white household. Using actual dollar amounts, a white family at the midpoint of the wealth range for white families has approximately $100,000, while a black family in the middle of the wealth range has approximately $7,000, and a Latino family has approximately $8,000. Asian American families tend to have the highest income of all racial groups, but their total wealth is approximately 70 percent of that of white families.[1] The fact that these racial wealth differences are so large means wealthy schools, neighborhoods, and environments tend to be disproportionately white, while lower-income ones are often disproportionately African American and Latino.

Racial inequalities affect children at the earliest stages of their education. They also affect the relationship between a person's education and his or her earning potential. Many people think of graduating from high school and completing college as essential to a high-income career. In 2014, Abigail Bessler reported for *ThinkProgress* on differences in hiring between blacks and whites in terms of education. The title of her article expresses the disparity: "A Black College Student Has the Same Chances of Getting a Job as a White High School Dropout."[2] Bessler reported findings by Young Invincibles, an organization committed to empowering young people in the political process, which analyzed government labor and census data and found

THE BLACK PANTHERS AND FREE BREAKFAST

The Black Panthers were an activist group, most prominent in the 1960s and 1970s, whose members believed black people in America should fight injustice by seeking self-determination, pride, and power. They rejected the idea that they should wait for the government to give more civil rights to minorities and focused on community empowerment instead. In 1968, the Black Panthers began a free breakfast program for public school children in a majority black neighborhood of Oakland, California. After a year, the group expanded the program to include free breakfast for 20,000 schoolchildren across the country.[3] The goal of the program was to feed children who might not have enough food to eat at home, helping them start the school day with a full stomach and the ability to concentrate and learn.

The Employment Gap[4]

Education does little to close the gap between black males and their white counterparts until the highest levels of education.

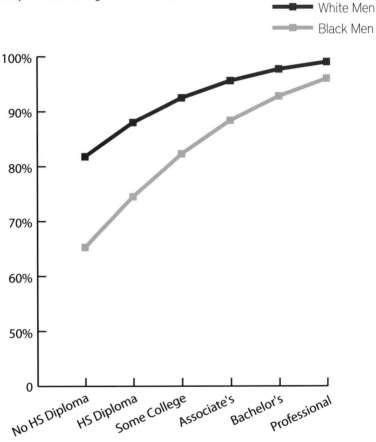

that at every level of education, black people were hired for jobs at lower rates than white people with the same amount of education. This means high school and higher education do not give the same boost to people of every race.

GENDER

Educational opportunity also affects men and women differently. For much of US history, it was uncommon for women to be highly educated. Many people thought women were less intellectually capable than men and did not need to prepare for careers like men did. Today, women graduate from high school, two-year associate's degree programs, and four-year bachelor's degree programs at higher rates than men do. This is true for women of all races.

However, evidence from the National Center for Education Statistics shows that women tend to have less wealth and income than men. This is the case even when women achieve well in school. More women than men are living below the poverty line. And women, on average, make less money than men, regardless of their jobs. In other words, while educational access for women and racial minorities has improved over time, that access has not ended some long-existing wealth gaps.

GIRLS AND THE MATH GAP

Research shows that at the beginning of kindergarten, boys and girls tend to have similar math skills. But by the end of elementary school, boys tend to score better than girls on math tests. Some scientists have suggested that one reason for the gap is that teachers tend to think of boys as being better at math than girls, even when they are not. A 2016 study published by the American Educational Research Association showed that when teachers were asked to judge their students' math abilities, they rated boys higher than girls who had equal grades and scores.

DISABILITIES

America also has a long history of excluding people with disabilities from the structures of the education system. In the 1800s, a common practice was for families to send children with physical disabilities, such as deafness or blindness, or children who were labeled "feebleminded," to special institutions.[5] This isolated them from the rest of the world.

In the early 1900s, immigrant children and English-language learners of low socioeconomic status were often placed in special classes for students with disabilities. In the 1960s and 1970s, the federal government and the disability rights movement started to recognize the education system needed to understand disabilities better and work on behalf of disabled children.

As public understanding of disabilities has evolved, the laws protecting the educational opportunities of people with disabilities have evolved, too. Three main laws help ensure that children with disabilities receive equal treatment at school and in other public places. These laws are the Americans with Disabilities Act, the Individuals with Disabilities Education Act, and Section 504. They protect students from discrimination and help them get the resources they need in the classroom. However, schools across the United States can receive very different amounts of money to spend on children with disabilities. This means that not every child in public school who has a disability has the same amount of access to help and services.

The special education system and the exclusion and lack of services that can come with it intersect with race. Children of color are overrepresented in special education classes. Children with disabilities are supposed to be placed in mainstream public school classes as often as possible. This means children of color are more likely to be placed in separate special education classes than white children. In other words, the structures of disability-based separation and race-based separation overlap in special education classrooms.

In addition, while public schools are required to accommodate students with disabilities, private and charter schools do not necessarily have to follow the same rules.

This means that while students with disabilities are now a part of the structure of public education, the structures of private and charter schools can leave them out.

LANGUAGE

Language is also related to the structures of class in the United States. English is the standard teaching and learning language across the vast majority of the country, as well as the language used most in powerful sectors such as business and politics. Public school curricula, or plans for learning and instruction, are designed and taught in English. And English reading and writing

Sixth graders in Mount Vernon, Washington, play a video they made about growing up in a bilingual world. They hope to inspire others.

are considered fundamental learning skills. In addition, research in *Social Science Medicine* shows that the ability to speak English fluently boosts both social status and earning potential in the United States.

English-language learners have the extra task of adapting to English in order to adapt to the US class and education systems. Many students who are English-language learners come from working-class and impoverished backgrounds. Approximately two-thirds of these students come from low-income families.[6] As a result, in addition to the challenge of learning English, these young people also face the struggles presented by being in low socioeconomic classes.

EARLY BILINGUAL EDUCATION

Many young children grow up learning more than one language at the same time. Some kids grow up speaking one language with their families and another one at school. Others might speak different languages with different family members. In the past, some researchers thought bilingual education kept students from learning properly. Later research showed that learning two languages at a young age improves kids' thinking in several ways, such as providing them a better understanding of the structure of languages and a better ability to concentrate deeply in order to solve problems.

INDIVIDUAL PERSPECTIVE

One of the struggles students from lower classes face is feeling a part of the school experience, as though they belong to it and deserve what it offers. University of Pennsylvania researcher

Annette Lareau studied a group of middle school students of various races and socioeconomic backgrounds. She found a major difference between middle-class and low-income children.

Lareau explained that middle-class children tended to feel they belonged at school and were entitled, or had a right to, attention from their teachers and help with their desires and needs. Children from low-income backgrounds had a different experience. They felt disengaged, less at home in school, and more separate from their teachers. According to Lareau, these students felt disengaged because they felt as though the structure of the school was working against them. These attitudes can have a lifelong impact on children's education, affecting their educational goals and the relationships they form with teachers and other school figures.

DISCUSSION STARTERS

- Why do you think women tend to make less money than men in the workplace even though they are more likely to graduate from high school and college? If you were a lawmaker, how would you address this issue?

- How do you think classrooms could be made more accessible to all students?

- What do you think it means to feel "entitled" and to feel "disengaged"? What are some things you feel entitled to at school?

FOUR

CLASS AND THE
PUBLIC SCHOOL
SYSTEM

P ublic schools offer equal opportunity in that they are open to all children. However, the opportunities available, such as having the latest technology—or even sufficient school supplies or adequate facilities—are not the same from school to school. The structure of public schooling supports an unequal class system. It is one that highlights the cultural and individual effects of class on the learning experience.

SCHOOL FUNDING

As of 2017, almost 51 million students attended public elementary and secondary schools in the United States.[1] That equates to approximately 90 percent of students.[2] Every US state requires students to go to school. The mandatory ages of

Public school students from Jackson, Mississippi, spoke about resource struggles at their schools at the state capitol in February 2018.

attendance vary from state to state. For instance, in Pennsylvania, school attendance is mandatory from age 8 to age 17, while Utah requires attendance from age 6 to age 18. The standard ages of school attendance are from 5, when kids go to kindergarten, to 18, when they graduate from high school.

While all children have the right (and the obligation) to get an education, they do not have the right to the same amount of money for school. Funding for public schools comes from three main sources. Approximately 9 percent is from the federal government and 46 percent comes from local governments, with the rest of the money coming from the state.[3] States play a large role in setting educational rules such as mandatory attendance and curricula. Local governments, which decide on school districts and set school policy through an elected school board, also greatly influence how public schools are run.

Local school districts typically raise money for their schools through property taxes, which are taxes on local homes and businesses. Because wealthy people tend to have more expensive homes, rich neighborhoods can collect more money in property taxes and spend that money on their schools. This means there are often huge differences between the money spent on public schools in low-income areas versus high-income areas. On average, US public schools spend approximately $12,000 per year per student on education. Some districts, however, spend almost three times that per student.[4] Differences in funding affect things such as teacher salaries, building quality and safety, materials such as new textbooks and laboratory supplies, and funding for electives and arts programs.

EFFECTS OF UNEQUAL FUNDING

One example of how these differences in funding affect schools and students comes from Connecticut. On average, Connecticut students score well in national standardized tests. But there are huge differences between the scores of high-income and low-income students. In 2016, the *New York Times* reported on two very different Connecticut towns. In Fairfield, many students come from upper-middle-class socioeconomic backgrounds, and most residents are white. More than 90 percent of students graduate from high school on time.[5] In nearby Bridgeport, where the average income is much lower and most residents are African-American or Latino, 63 percent of high school students graduate on time, and the school district suffers from shortages of

TEACHERS PAY FOR SCHOOL SUPPLIES

Many school districts have difficulty getting the books and supplies they need for their classrooms. A 2016 survey sponsored by the educational publishing company Scholastic polled 4,721 public educators.[6] Responses revealed that the majority of public school teachers spend their own money on books for their classrooms. The survey also found that in high-poverty schools, school teachers spend approximately twice as much of their own money on school supplies than teachers in low-poverty schools.[7]

supplies and necessities, such as buses.[8] The Bridgeport school district spends $2,000 less per student than Fairfield does.[9] Unlike the high-income families in Fairfield, Bridgeport families cannot afford to spend extra money when the school budget falls short.

In 2016, Connecticut judge Thomas Moukawsher ruled on a case that called the state's unequal funding of schools unconstitutional. Although he did not go so far as to rule against the entire funding system, he said that "change must come" and gave the state 180 days to review its school funding policies.[10] In 2017, there was a proposal to take $300 million from middle- and high-income school districts and give it to the poorest school districts. But the proposal did not make it into the state budget. The budget for 2018 did include an increase of $30 million for education and a change to the formula Connecticut uses to allocate money that will result in more dollars going to districts with greater need.[11]

CLASS AND CULTURE

Class differences between students in schools are a form of diversity, and that diversity can be a good thing. Evidence shows that socioeconomically diverse schools help students. In 2016, the Century Foundation, a research organization, found that "when a school reaches a stable level of about 30 percent middle-class students, the lower-income students achieve at higher levels and the privileged students do no worse."[12] In other words, class diversity can help students do well in school.

However, differences in socioeconomic status can also mean differences in opportunities for education and activity outside the classroom. Public schools often expect students and their families to contribute money for sports supplies, class trips, and other extracurricular activities. This can place an extra burden on low-income families, which may not have enough money to pay these expenses. In addition, some children and teens need to watch siblings, help their families, or work after school and do not have time to enroll in extracurricular activities. For these reasons, middle- and high-income students are more likely to participate in school clubs and sports, a difference experts call "the activity gap."[13]

Socioeconomic differences can also be a source of stress and tension for students in other areas related to school. School lunch is one of them. Most public schools have cafeterias where children can pay to eat lunch. Children whose families do not have enough money to buy lunch can enroll in free or reduced-price lunch programs. As of 2016, approximately 30 million children participated

ARTS FUNDING IN PUBLIC SCHOOLS

Research shows that students who receive an arts education tend to do better in school and are less likely to get in trouble outside of school. Nevertheless, many struggling schools cut their arts programs because of underfunding or debt. In 2017, musical artist Chance the Rapper, concerned about the quality of arts programs at public schools in his native Chicago, Illinois, raised $2.2 million to help Chicago's public schools. In addition, he donated $1 million of his own money to support public school arts programs.[14]

In 2017, second graders got lunch at school in Santa Fe, New Mexico, where all public school students are offered the same lunch to avoid lunch shaming.

in such programs.[15] However, some schools have taken a hard stance against students whose families cannot pay for lunch. In 2017, a cafeteria worker at a school in Minnesota shamed students because their families owed money for school meals. The worker took food off the students' lunch trays and put it in a bucket. Minnesota politician Sarah Anderson condemned the behavior, saying, "It's school-sanctioned bullying of children. It's not their fault."[16] Brenda Cassellius, Minnesota's education commissioner, also spoke out against this treatment: "Taking food away from a child in front of their peers, or limiting their access to school activities or athletics over meal debt, is downright wrong—not to mention mean."[17]

Clothing can be another sign of class status and source of stress. Some public schools have

introduced school uniforms. The thought behind the practice is that having all students wear the same clothes to school will help reduce class-based bullying. On the other hand, some people think the uniforms do not allow students to take pride in their differences and express themselves.

SAN ANTONIO INDEPENDENT PUBLIC SCHOOL DISTRICT V. RODRIGUEZ

In 1971, Demetrio Rodriguez decided to take action against what he saw as the injustice of the local public school system. Rodriguez's children went to a public school in San Antonio, Texas. The school lacked good textbooks and was in a cramped building. The children in the next neighborhood had new supplies and plenty of space. Rodriguez's case went to the US Supreme Court, arguing that all children in a public school deserved adequate funding. He lost. In a 5–4 ruling in 1973, the justices argued that education is not a fundamental right and, therefore, not everyone deserves a certain amount of funding for their education.

FIXING THE ACHIEVEMENT GAP

Student socioeconomic background and public school funding are related to graduation and academic success. Students from low-income backgrounds are less likely to graduate from high school than wealthier students. Research shows that states that give more money to their lowest-income schools sometimes improve student test scores at those schools.

It is clear that changing the structure of school funding by giving more money to low-income schools can lead

LUNCH SHAMING

In most public school districts, students have to pay money to eat lunch at the school cafeteria. Seventy-five percent of school districts have debt from unpaid school lunch accounts.[18] To collect that money, some school districts practice lunch shaming, where children with school lunch debt are given cold sandwiches instead of a hot meal or branded with a stamp that shows they owe money. In a few districts, children with student lunch debt get no lunch at all. Approximately one-half of school districts with school lunch debt shame their students.

Many people criticize lunch shaming, arguing that it embarrasses children whose parents cannot afford to pay bills and punishes them by denying them a satisfying hot lunch. Others argue that lunch shaming motivates parents to pay their child's bills. The US Department of Agriculture discourages school districts from lunch shaming. And some cities, such as Detroit, Michigan, and Boston, Massachusetts, give free lunches to all students.

to improvements. However, studies also show that some of the achievement differences between lower-income and higher-income students are due to factors that are related to class but outside of a school's control. Class affects children in many ways before they even walk through the door of a school. Students who live in poverty experience more stress and more life obstacles than students who do not. This can include not having enough food to eat or being homeless. These stresses can have a lifelong negative effect on a child's physical and mental health. These factors can damage students' ability to learn, even in a high-quality school with good teachers.

American culture is full of stories about education lifting people out of poverty, and many proposed reforms to the education system assume that a good education will always help students of lower socioeconomic status. It is also useful, though, to consider the ways in which the effects of poverty can overcome the benefits of education.

DISCUSSION STARTERS

- What do you think public schools should do to fix the activity gap?

- Imagine your school had $50,000 more each year to spend on students. What should the school spend it on?

- Do you think public school students should wear uniforms? Why or why not?

PRIVATE SCHOOLS AND
HOMESCHOOLING

A pproximately 10 percent of all elementary, middle, and high school students in the United States attend private schools.[1] Private schools are not funded by government money and typically meet their expenses by charging tuition to students. The average annual tuition of private schools ranges between $7,000 and $13,000 per year, depending on the type of school and the grade level.[2] This structural difference is the most important difference between public and private schools.

FUNDING, POPULATION, AND PERFORMANCE

Although many private schools offer some scholarships or grants to low-income students, private schools can refuse to let

The money private schools get from charging tuition allows them to provide computers and other resources important for educating children.

In January 2018, students from charter, private, parochial, and home schools participated in a rally in Jackson, Mississippi, in support of school choice.

in anyone whose family cannot pay the tuition fee. In general, private schools are smaller than public schools, with fewer students overall and more teachers per student. Private schools have to obey some, but not all, of the state education laws that public schools do. For example, while all public school teachers need to be certified by the state to teach, not all states have the same requirement for private school teachers.

In general, a higher percentage of private school students are of high socioeconomic status than public school students. Private school students tend to score better than public school students in most tests of academic achievement. However, some researchers think the difference is due to the type of student, not the type of school. In other words, research suggests that private school students do better because they tend to be richer to begin with and receive the early and ongoing benefits of higher socioeconomic status.

Critics of private schools say they make income inequality worse by giving extra resources, time, and attention to students who are already rich. Others point out that private schools reduce the socioeconomic diversity of the schools in their neighborhoods and that students miss out on this diversity. Some people have called for private schools to be taxed instead of treated like nonprofits and not taxed. They argue that this would help reduce the inequalities between public and private education because the money from property taxes on nonprofit private schools could be used for the public school system.

ELITE SCHOOLS AND THE CULTURE OF PRIVATE EDUCATION

There are a few elite private schools in the United States. These schools are selective and expensive. They are often boarding schools and attract very wealthy families.

Phillips Academy in Andover, Massachusetts, is an elite high school. It was founded in 1778. The cost per student per year is $53,900 for boarding students and $41,900 for daytime students.[3] The amount is greater than the total yearly income of a low-class household and greater than that of some middle-class earners. Close to one-half of all Phillips students receive some financial aid. Thirteen percent of students get full scholarships to the school.[4] While the student body has some class diversity, the high cost of tuition means wealthy students are overrepresented.

Like many wealthy private schools, Phillips Academy offers learning opportunities beyond those of the typical public school. Phillips has classes in Japanese and Arabic and an archaeology center. Two US presidents, George H. W. Bush and George W. Bush, attended the school. Going to an elite private school helps students get into selective colleges. A study by the *Harvard Crimson*, Harvard University's school newspaper, found that 1 in 20 Harvard students came from the same seven schools, five of which were elite private schools and two of which were public schools.[5]

The class culture of elite private schools can be stressful and lonely for students from low- and middle-income backgrounds. The *New York Times* reported in 2012 on the ways

FOR-PROFIT VERSUS NONPROFIT PRIVATE SCHOOLS

Most private schools in the United States are considered nonprofit organizations. This means they do not have to pay federal, state, or local taxes. Also, they can accept donations of charity to help with their expenses. A smaller number of private schools are run as for-profit operations. While a nonprofit school has a board of directors that helps make decisions, for-profit schools can be run by corporations or even only one person.

children from low-income families can feel out of step at elite schools. The article featured D. J. Banton, who attended Trinity, a private school in New York. Banton said, "The differences were in money and in the way I was raised. . . . I had never been to camp, and I couldn't change or control that."[6]

RELIGIOUS SCHOOLS

The majority of US private schools are religious schools, combining traditional education with the lessons and values of a particular faith. Catholic schools are the biggest subset

PRIVATE TUTORING

In past centuries, it was common practice in European and North American cultures for wealthy people to educate their children with the help of private tutors who lived in the home of the family that employed them. Today, families can hire private tutors to help with homework, test preparation, or any subjects a student might need help with. Plenty of nonprofits and public libraries offer tutoring to students of all income levels. Companies such as Kumon Learning Centers operate large tutoring centers where groups of students can study after school. These services can cost $100 a month, making them accessible for middle-income students.[7] Considerably more expensive tutors also exist. In 2013, former high school teacher Nathaniel Hannan admitted that he can make up to $1,250 an hour as a private tutor for extremely wealthy clients.[8] Private tutors like Hannan often get perks as well, such as free room and board, a car or someone to drive them, and free travel. Hannan described his experience: "We have to get results with these kids. That's a great deal of pressure on us. I'm working with kids who really need me and I make a significant difference for those children, and it's what I want to do with my life, so it's great."[9]

of religious private education, representing approximately 40 percent of all private schools.[10]

Historically, the tuition rates of Catholic schools have been lower than those of other types of private schools. Today, average tuition at a Catholic elementary school is approximately $4,000, and almost all Catholic schools give financial aid to students.[11] Catholic schools used to be seen as affordable private school options for middle-income families or low-to-no-cost school choices for low-income families. However, many Catholic schools have closed in the past few decades. The change may have to do with changes in cities' religious populations as well as rising tuition in Catholic schools.

The United States is also home to significant numbers of Protestant Christian, Jewish, and Islamic private schools. For example, at the private Al Fatih elementary and middle school in Reston, Virginia, students take

HISTORY OF CATHOLIC EDUCATION

Catholic schools, colleges, and universities have a long international history. Catholic priests and nuns often choose a career in education as a way to do charity or missionary work. The first Catholic school in America was created in 1606 in Florida with the goal of converting Native Americans to Catholicism. The first Catholic charity school, a school for poor girls, opened in New Orleans in 1727. In the 1800s, many parish schools opened to serve Catholic immigrants from other countries. Today, approximately two million US children attend Catholic schools, and a little over 80 percent of them are from Catholic backgrounds.[12]

Third graders at St. Gregory Cathedral School, a Catholic school in Texas, took part in a "Brain Break" dance on the first day of the 2016–2017 school year.

Arabic lessons and learn about the values of the Islamic faith alongside lessons in history, science, and civics.

HOMESCHOOLING

US education options include more than public and private schools. Approximately 3 percent of American families homeschool their children.[13] Homeschooling is when children are schooled at home. Parents teach from a set curriculum, parents teach according to their own values and standards, or groups of famllies get together to teach their kids in small groups.

Laws on homeschooling vary from state to state. Most states require homeschoolers to teach children certain subjects, but only some of the states test homeschooled students or evaluate homeschool classrooms to see what children learn. Most of the states that do have assessments have no consequences for

poor results. The vast majority of homeschooling families say one of the reasons they make the choice to homeschool is because they are concerned about the school environment.

The socioeconomic demographics of homeschooled students are similar to those of public school students, although homeschoolers are more likely to be white and to have a parent with a bachelor's degree. Some critics say that, like private schooling, homeschooling takes students out of the public school system and has a negative effect on school diversity.

DISCUSSION STARTERS

- Why do you think children in private schools tend to do better on tests than children in public schools? Give a few reasons.

- Should religious education and academic education be combined or separate? Explain your answer.

- Do you think homeschooled students should have to learn the same subjects as public school students? What about private school students?

- Do you think it's important for children to go to school with people of different class backgrounds? Why or why not?

SIX

STRATEGIES FOR
CHANGING US
SCHOOLING

M any families, educators, and policymakers want to combine private and public education in various ways. Magnet schools, charter schools, and the voucher system are three strategies for changing the structure of schooling in the United States. All of these ideas have passionate supporters and critics.

CHARTER SCHOOLS

A charter school is a school that is supported through a mix of public and private funds. Like traditional public schools, charter schools do not charge tuition. Unlike a public school, a charter school has a board of directors. The board's members represent

In 2016, the Thompson family checked to see if Jada would attend first grade at Neighborhood House Charter School in Boston, Massachusetts.

the private backers of the school and can help make decisions about hiring, firing, and curriculum.

Charter schools are usually considered to be a type of public school, but they do receive private money. And the people who give that money are allowed to have a great amount of influence over how the school is run.

Charter schools have a long history. The academies of the colonial period were often funded by a mix of corporate and state money. In 1855, the United States had approximately 6,000 academies, many of them in the South. Today, approximately 6,750 charter schools are operating, and they make up approximately 7 percent of public schools.[1]

The arguments for and against charter schools are closely related to class. Many supporters believe these schools can bring new funding, experimental educational methods, and better academic

---

WAITING FOR SUPERMAN

In 2010, Davis Guggenheim, an Oscar-winning documentary filmmaker, released a documentary called *Waiting for Superman*. In the film, Guggenheim explored what he saw as the failures of the public school system. The documentary follows five children who attend public schools but are hoping to go to charter schools. At the end of the movie, most of the children do not win the charter school lottery. Only one is accepted into a charter school, while another gets into a private school. Movie critics and school reform advocates liked the film, but teachers unions and representatives criticized what they saw as unfair bias against public schools.

performance to low-income areas. Eva Moskowitz, the head of a well-known chain of New York charter schools called Success Academy, said,

> I think it's fairly unique to define the end goal of K–12 schooling as helping students become better thinkers, more creative thinkers, and to organize the whole school around creative and critical thinking. That's not how most schools in America would describe their mission.[2]

Moskowitz is critical of the culture of the traditional public school system, saying it does not push students to think. She speaks out against certain aspects of public schooling, such as contracts that allow teachers to stay in their jobs even if they

CHARTER SCHOOLS AND DISCIPLINE

In recent years, some charter schools have developed very strict approaches to school discipline. These strategies are often called "no excuses" policies, and they are meant to boost student achievement by setting high, strict standards for students in the classroom.[3] For example, Carver Collegiate Academy, one of many charter schools in New Orleans, Louisiana, demands that students say "thank you" every time they are called on in class. They must walk in taped paths marked in the hallways. Advocates of strict charter schools say they can create structured, focused environments that help low-income students gain an advantage. Others argue that this approach teaches already vulnerable students that they are problems and potential troublemakers, leading them to dread school or drop out. These critics think singling out low-income and minority children for strict treatment is unfair. They argue that this type of school climate is very different from the luxury atmosphere of elite private schools.

perform poorly. She thinks the existing system does not do enough to improve flawed public schools.

Success Academy, like other charter schools, runs admissions through a lottery system. Families fill out a very short application, describing where they live and the age of their child, and submit it to the school by April 1. The school selects students from those applications until it has filled all its spots, giving some preferences, such as to children of employees and to children with siblings already at the school. Success Academy has had a track record of improving test scores and performance for its students, most of whom live in low-income neighborhoods. However, it has been accused of failing to help students with disabilities and of working to push out students it considers difficult. In fact, charter schools tend to enroll fewer English-language learners and students with disabilities than similar public schools.

KIPP

Knowledge Is Power Program (KIPP) is a network of charter schools with locations across the continental United States. The program began in 1994 with one school in Houston, Texas. Today, 209 K–12 schools serve mostly low-income students.[4]

A 2013 study by Mathematica Policy Research showed that KIPP students tend to make more learning gains than public school students. KIPP also stands out for its culture of discipline, a common trait for charter schools. KIPP's students walk single file between classes and get demerits for leaning against a wall. A 2016 CityLab study showed that some KIPP schools have some of the highest rates of "discipline incidents," including suspension and expulsion.[5]

Eager students at KIPP Memphis Collegiate Middle School in Tennessee held up their work in writing class on October 5, 2012.

Despite Success Academy's track record of high test scores, evidence about the effectiveness of charter schools is mixed. Stanford University's Center for Research in Education Outcomes studied data from 15 states and the District of Columbia. The data represented 70 percent of the nation's charter schools.[6] Researchers found that, in the long run, switching to a charter school does not necessarily improve a child's academic ability. Some researchers think charter schools in cities work well, whereas charter schools in suburban areas do not. In Michigan, where many charter schools are run by for-profit companies, journalists found examples of corruption and wasted money at many locations. Michigan had more charter schools than public schools perform poorly.

MAGNET SCHOOLS

After *Brown v. Board of Education* (1954) ended legal school segregation, some school districts were faced with a problem. Many white families resisted desegregation and tried to avoid sending their children to schools with large numbers of racial minorities. Many white parents moved out of districts if they knew their children would be sent to integrated schools, taking their money and resources with them. This trend was known as "white flight."[7]

Magnet schools were proposed as a way to integrate schools while avoiding white flight. A magnet school is a public school that hosts a special program. Unlike charter schools, magnet schools are funded entirely with public money and have to follow state education laws. Magnet schools can attract students from near and far, bringing in students from other parts of a school district. These schools attempted to change the culture and diversity of some public schools without making larger changes to the ways public schools are funded.

In 1971, the US Supreme Court's decision in *Swann v. Charlotte-Mecklenburg Board of Education* allowed public school districts to convert schools in low-income, majority-black areas into magnet schools to attract white students. In 2017, the United States had more than 4,000 magnet schools.[8] Some of the most common types of magnet schools are science, technology, engineering, and mathematics (STEM) schools and performing

Lashawn Robinson, *right*, and other parents filed a lawsuit in 2018 saying race-based student quotas at magnet schools in Hartford, Connecticut, were unlawful and have kept students, including her son, *left*, from attending.

arts schools. Initially, magnet schools successfully increased racial and ethnic diversity in schools. In 2015, a study by the American Institutes of Research showed that turning a public school into a magnet school does not necessarily increase socioeconomic diversity, although it tends to increase racial diversity.

VOUCHERS

Some people believe the traditional public school system does not provide students and families with the choices they need. These critics of public schools think families should have the power to choose what to do with the money the government spends on their children's educations. They think the funding

Residents waited to speak during a school board meeting in Colorado in 2017. The board was set to end a program to help public school students attend secular and religious schools with taxpayer-funded vouchers.

structure of the public education system should change. Instead of public money going directly to schools, it should go to students and their families.

Fifteen US states and the District of Columbia offer voucher programs. Through these programs, some families can receive special grants of government money, known as vouchers, to spend on their child's private education. Some of these programs are designed for children in low-income families or children with disabilities who may need specialized services.

Voucher supporters say the programs help gifted low-income children get a high-quality public education. They believe the ability to choose a school is an important type of freedom and public schools will improve if they are forced to compete with private schools for students.

Voucher critics think government money should be spent improving public schools for all students. They point out that most private schools are religious, even though public education is typically supposed to separate church and state. Other critics argue that voucher programs cannot do enough to help poor students because the amount of the voucher is often not enough to cover the full cost of tuition at a private school. In addition, families of children with disabilities who use voucher money to move to a private school may lose their protection under the Individuals with Disabilities Education Act. For example, special education services cost nothing to families in public school, but a private school may charge families. Little evidence exists showing voucher programs improve students' academic success.

DISCUSSION STARTERS

- Do you think charter schools should follow the same learning standards as public schools?

- Propose a magnet school for your school district. Which students would it teach, what area would it focus on, and how would it affect educational opportunities in your area?

- What's your opinion about school choice? Do you think all students should be able to choose their own school? Should it be available to some students? Or should all students attend public school?

SEVEN

CLASS AND
TEACHING

T eachers, along with principals and other school
administrators, make up a big piece of the class and
education puzzle. In the United States, teaching in public
school is a middle-class profession. Many teachers have to think
about the mental and emotional effects of socioeconomic
differences in their classrooms. And they have to stay aware of
the class differences between themselves and their students.
Recent attempts at teaching reform have focused on improving
teachers at low-income schools, helping good teachers get
better and firing bad teachers more quickly. But this approach
may not be enough to get at the deeper structural problems
within the public education system.

Regardless of the school, good teachers
are critical.

THE STRUCTURE OF THE TEACHING PROFESSION

Teaching is a very common job, with more than three million public school teachers working in the United States in 2017.[1] The average US salary for school teachers is approximately $56,000, making teaching a solidly middle-class job, with a salary that is somewhat higher than that of most jobs.[2] Teaching in a private school tends to pay less than teaching in public schools.

The majority of teachers have a college degree or higher. In the public school system, teacher salary is based on age and teaching experience, not on other factors, so that teachers in high-need or challenging teaching situations do not get more money than teachers with less stressful jobs.

CLASS, CULTURE, AND THE CLASSROOM

In the early days of the United States, teaching was mainly a job for young men. In the mid-1800s, that changed. Education reformers such as Horace Mann and John Dewey tended to hire women because they thought women had natural caring and sympathy that made them better teachers.

Because women could be paid less than men, school administrators were able to save money by hiring female staff. Teaching is still a female-dominated profession. According to the National Center for Education Statistics, during the 2011–2012 school year, approximately 75 percent of public school teachers were women.[3] The teaching profession is also mostly white, at approximately 80 percent.[4]

While American teachers tend to be middle class, female, and white, the classrooms of the country are more diverse. A majority of US public school students are not white, and students come from all socioeconomic backgrounds. Successful teachers must be aware of how differences in socioeconomic class may affect how children approach school. They also need to be aware of how comfortable children feel in the classroom.

Resources are available to help teachers tackle issues of socioeconomic class in their lessons. For example, the American Psychological Association recommends that teachers use group activities and lessons to talk about issues of class diversity and bias with their students. In one exercise, students read about the life

NYC MEN TEACH

Some nonprofits and local governments are working to recruit more men of color to work as public K–12 teachers. In New York City, where 43 percent of students are nonwhite males and only 8 percent of teachers are, NYC Men Teach is working to change that.[5] The city government program is holding workshops and traveling across the country to find men of color to work in New York City schools. Some of these men may not have considered teaching as a career. The program aims to convince men of color that they are needed in the classroom. Supporters of the program think male teachers of color can serve as role models in the classroom, empathizing with students and adding their valuable perspectives and life experiences to the teaching environment.

experiences of a group of low-income and middle-income women and think about and discuss how their own experiences might be similar or different.

CLASS AND TEACHING REFORM

Teachers at low-income schools are often lower-rated than teachers at high-income schools. Some bold school-reform plans have concentrated on getting rid of bad teachers. Michelle Rhee got a lot of publicity for her plan to reform public schools in Washington, DC, when she was school chancellor and head of the school system. Rhee became a teacher after participating in Teach for America, a program that hires recent college graduates to work as teachers in underprivileged schools.

When she became school chancellor in 2007, Rhee decided to close more than 20 schools that were not successfully educating kids.[6] Rhee also changed teacher contracts so that it was easier to fire teachers who did not help raise their students' test scores. The contract also connected a teacher's salary to his or her

ANTIBIAS EDUCATION

Some educators think teaching children to value diversity is important. They want children to learn to challenge negative stereotypes about people from other backgrounds. Antibias education uses a variety of strategies to help students develop pride in their own backgrounds and recognize prejudice or unfairness. The strategies include guided class discussions, books on diversity and inclusion, and lessons on cultural diversity, such as learning about a variety of religious holidays.

ability to raise test scores. Effective teachers would get more money and consistently low-performing teachers could be fired. Rhee's policies upset teachers and their labor unions. These teachers felt that judging them only by student test scores was unfair because some students would take longer to improve.

In 2010, Rhee left her job after voters in Washington, DC, elected a new mayor. Years after her departure, her approach to reform is still controversial, and experts do not agree on her legacy. One 2017 analysis from *US News & World Report* shows that between 2007 and 2015, math and reading scores of students in District of Columbia public schools increased.

STAND AND DELIVER

Many films, books, and stories about teachers reflect the cultural belief that an extraordinary teacher can have a large and lasting positive effect on the lives of disadvantaged students. One of the most famous movies about teaching excellence and social inequality, *Stand and Deliver*, is based on the true story of a high school math teacher in California. Jaime Escalante was a Bolivian-born teacher who worked in a low-income, majority-Latino high school in East Los Angeles in the 1970s and 1980s. He taught calculus, a subject some of his colleagues thought was too difficult for his students. In 1982, Escalante's advanced math students, inspired by his high-energy teaching style, attended extra math practice in the early mornings and on weekends. They all passed a college-level calculus exam. The film explains how testmakers, surprised by math mastery at a poor minority high school, were so suspicious of Escalante's students' high results that the students were forced to take the test again. Although some of Escalante's math students were high achievers under his guidance, he moved to another high school later in his career and did not have the same level of success.

THE TEACH FOR AMERICA
CONTROVERSY

Teach for America is a nonprofit organization with its own solution to the teacher problem in American schools. It hires college students with high grades and an interest in public service to work as teachers in low-income public schools for two years. The organization thinks these young, high-achieving teachers can inspire their students and make a difference in the field of education.

Participants do not usually have a degree in education, and they train for approximately five weeks before starting their jobs. Many drop out of the program early because they are overwhelmed by the needs of their classrooms. The majority of people who complete their two years stay in the teaching field, but most leave the low-income schools where they begin their careers.

Some educators think having new, inexperienced teachers work in underfunded schools increases inequality instead of working to fix it. Career teachers worry that, because participants work for lower salaries, the program hurts teachers' ability to negotiate for more money and better working conditions. Others argue that Teach for America helps recruit talented young people into the teaching profession, pointing out that some studies show that Teach for America graduates tend to make better-than-average math teachers.

Teach for America instructor Marissa Molina taught Spanish to students in Denver, Colorado, in 2014.

On October 19, 2016, thousands of New York City teachers rallied for more charter schools.

However, a *Washington Monthly* article points out that achievement gaps between low-income and high-income students widened.

THE IMPORTANCE OF TEACHERS

In addition to a lack of funds, resources, and supplies, students attending low-income schools are also more likely to have low-performing teachers. Journalist Dana Goldstein summarized a large body of research on the value individual teachers bring to education: "Effective teachers can narrow, but not close, achievement and employment gaps that reflect broader income, wealth, and racial inequalities in American society."[7]

In other words, an effective teacher who understands and motivates students can help raise their test scores and improve their learning. Still, nonschool issues, such as a student's emotional and mental health and ability to access healthy food, are all more important for school success than having a great teacher. Even the greatest teacher cannot make up for a student's lack of these important life needs.

DISCUSSION STARTERS

- Do you think teachers should be paid more than they are now? Why or why not?

- Imagine you are a second-grade teacher. How would you discuss the idea of socioeconomic class with your students?

- Imagine you are a high school principal. What kind of teachers would you want to hire for your school? What strategies would you use to keep them from leaving their jobs?

CLASS AND HIGHER
EDUCATION

On November 12, 2015, college students from all over the the United States, at more than 100 campuses, came together to protest for themselves.[1] They argued for a major structural change in the US higher education system: free tuition. They also spoke out against low wages for campus workers and other types of social inequality on campus. The protest gained media attention, with approximately 70,000 mentions on Twitter.[2] Many observers disagreed with the goals of the march. But the students were reacting to a well-known fact of college life. In the United States, college is very expensive, and debt is typical for college graduates.

Attending and graduating from college is a major achievement and one that has extra challenges for many students from lower classes.

In 2017, approximately 20 million Americans attended college or university.[3] A college degree can be a pathway to a middle- or upper-class job. However, college is difficult to prepare for, pay for, and finish. Additionally, class inequalities affect every stage of the higher education process.

CLASS AND COLLEGE APPLICATIONS

In 2016, students from higher-income backgrounds were approximately 16 percent more likely to enroll in college than students from lower-income backgrounds.[4] This difference in enrollment is related to the inequalities that persist throughout the K–12 education process and to issues with the application

CLASS AND AFFIRMATIVE ACTION

One ongoing debate in higher education is about affirmative action. The policy raises chances of admission for students from groups that have a history of being shut out from higher education. Most affirmative action policies are focused on gender or race, giving preferences to women or members of racial or other minorities. Some people argue that affirmative action policies should be based on family income rather than race because the income achievement gap in education is wider than the racial achievement gap. Advocates of income-based affirmative action argue that it will overlap with race-based affirmative action, increasing black and Latino enrollment at colleges and universities by targeting low-income students of all races. Others say that race-based affirmative action is necessary. They argue that the structural biases against racial minorities are still in place at many colleges and universities and shifting affirmative action to deal only with income will not get rid of racial inequality.

process itself. On the SAT, a test meant to measure college readiness, students from low-income families tend to score lower than students from high-income backgrounds. One possible reason is that wealthy students and families can afford to pay for test preparation classes, private tutors, and study materials, whereas students with less money may be less familiar with the structure of the SAT. Like most standardized tests, the SAT measures a few very different things—skills in reading, writing, and math. It is also an indicator of test-taking skills, such as process of elimination, time management, and recognizing question types. Test tutors and specialized books can help with test-taking skills and make a significant difference in a student's score.

Additionally, applying to college is an expensive process. Most colleges charge a fee to apply. And many students spend a lot of money visiting campuses so they can understand the

COLLEGE ADMISSIONS ESSAYS

Many US colleges and universities ask students to write a short personal essay that explains one of their skills, passions, ambitions, or personal life experiences. This essay can be a way for students to explain how their socioeconomic class background has affected their view of life and desire to learn. Students with enough money can choose to hire a consultant. Consultants help students write about something they know will grab the attention of an admissions committee. They can also help students edit and structure their work so it is polished and free of mistakes. Some of these consultants charge $150 an hour.[5]

pros and cons of different schools. For students without the money for this process, hundreds of dollars in application fees can be overwhelming. The process itself, including time spent on applications, recommendations, essays, and financial aid forms, can be overwhelming, too.

PAYING FOR COLLEGE

Paying for college is difficult for students of almost any socioeconomic status. According to the National Center for Education Statistics, "For the 2014–15 academic year, average

New York governor Andrew Cuomo signed a law making state college tuition free for many students on April 10, 2017.

annual current dollar prices for undergraduate tuition, fees, room, and board were estimated to be $16,188 at public institutions, $41,970 at private nonprofit institutions, and $23,372 at private for-profit institutions."[6] Students who cannot afford to pay all their tuition and living expenses can pay for college with a mixture of scholarships, grants, and loans.

To receive financial aid from the government, students fill out a form called the Free Application for Federal Student Aid (FAFSA). They provide information about their family income and ability to pay for college. College students do not have to pay back grants or scholarships, although they may have to follow certain rules in order to keep the money. For example, the Pell Grant is a federal funding program designed to help students from low-income backgrounds attend college. In the 2017–2018 school year, the maximum amount a student could receive from a Pell Grant was $5,920 per year.[7] To continue getting a Pell Grant, students must stay in school and

THE FREE TUITION MOVEMENT

In some parts of the United States, students, educators, and lawmakers are pushing to get rid of college tuition. In New York State, the Excelsior program will guarantee free college tuition to students whose families make up to $125,000 a year.[8] Tennessee and Oregon have started initiatives to make community college free for their students. In October 2017, California made the first year of community college free. In 2013, a group of educators and business leaders began the Campaign for Free College Tuition, which conducts research and advocacy with the goal of getting rid of college tuition costs.

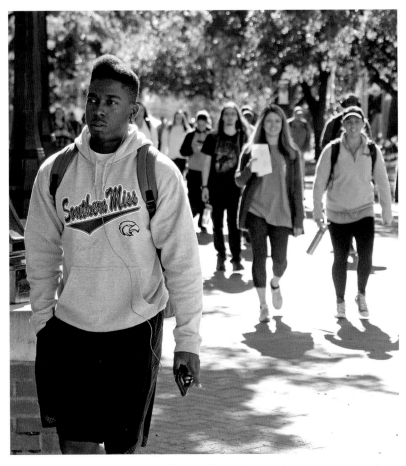

While students in some states will enjoy free tuition, others at state schools such as the University of Southern Mississippi face tuition increases.

keep a minimum grade point average that varies by school and is usually a 2.0 out of 4.0.

If students or families still cannot pay for college with their own money, scholarships, and grants, they can take out loans from the government or private banks. Student loans build up interest over time. This means that students must pay back more than they borrow, and many graduates start their careers with the burden of student loan debt. In 2017, the average student loan debt per graduate was greater than $17,000.[9]

Tuition costs are not the whole picture of the cost of college attendance. Students also have to take care of food, housing, school supplies, and other necessities when they are in school. College students with low socioeconomic status are more likely to have jobs while in school than students with high socioeconomic status. These jobs put more demands on these students' time and energy, making school more difficult. And students who work often have to balance low-paying or unsteady work with the demands of their college course work.

CLASS IN THE COLLEGE CLASSROOM

Class differences can affect the learning environments of college classrooms. Just as in K–12 public and private schools, the cultural environments of colleges can be unwelcoming to students from low-income backgrounds.

In 2009, the *Journal of Diversity in Higher Education* reported that students of low-class status were more likely to experience class discrimination on campus. Those experiences made them more likely to feel like they did not belong, less likely to feel healthy, and more likely to want to leave school.

COLLEGE EDUCATION AND CLASS STATUS

Plenty of people become successful and wealthy without a college degree. However, a college education is commonly associated with jobs that are considered middle and upper class. Employers offering white-collar jobs, which are middle-income office jobs, often seek out college graduates. In addition, many mid- to high-paying jobs, such as nurse, doctor, lawyer, and accountant, require a college education and sometimes a postgraduate degree.

The effect of a college education, and of class status in general, lasts over generations. College-educated people tend to marry and have children with other college-educated people. Often, college graduates live near each other in neighborhoods close to employers such as major companies, hospitals, and universities, and their combined wealth and property can help them fund local schools.

California's Silicon Valley is home to a large proportion of college graduates. Ever since powerful technology companies like Google put their headquarters there, the prices of houses in the area have skyrocketed. The test scores of children in the well-funded and high-quality Silicon Valley public schools are some of the highest in the country. And children of college-educated parents, such as the Silicon Valley parents, get an extra boost in their own college applications.

Google and other technology giants have changed Silicon Valley, including making it more expensive to live there. The upper-class region has top schools whose students get top scores on tests.

College-educated parents have the knowledge, experience, and connections to move their children effectively through the admissions process. Studies show that for applicants to elite private colleges and universities, being a legacy student, or someone whose parent went to the same school, gives a 23 percent admissions advantage.[10]

DISCUSSION STARTERS

- Do you think college admissions should be based on a standardized test? Why or why not?

- Some people think the most important function of a college degree is to help prepare students to find high-paying jobs. Do you agree? Why or why not?

- Many colleges offer legacy admissions policies, giving preference to applicants whose parents attended the college. What do you think of that idea?

NINE

LOOKING
AHEAD

I n the United States, the gap in school achievement between
rich and poor students starts early and grows over time. Many
education reformers believe the current education system
is simply unable to address this problem. Some of the biggest
pushes for school reform have come from people at the very top
of the socioeconomic class system. Billionaires have the money
and power to make changes to the structure of education.
However, they often lack a deep understanding of the cultural
and individual relationships between class and education.

Bill Gates started a foundation to confront a
variety of issues, including growing inequality in
the United States.

BILLIONAIRES AND EDUCATION REFORM

Bill Gates, the founder of Microsoft and one of the richest people in America, had a net worth of more than $90 billion at the end of 2017.[1] Gates is interested in reforming the US public education system. Through his organization, the Bill and Melinda Gates Foundation, Gates has pledged to spend up to $1.7 billion on initiatives for strengthening the public school system.[2]

Gates was a strong supporter of the Common Core State Standards, an attempt to get students ready for college by giving all US students the same expectations for achievement at the end of each grade. Gates invested hundreds of millions of dollars in the program, but its rollout had several problems. The people responsible for making Common Core happen underestimated how difficult it would be to set a new curriculum nationwide. Many parents and educators pushed back, complaining the curriculum had been put into place too quickly, without a good process in place to make sure it was proven to work.

Facebook founder Mark Zuckerberg, who had a net worth of more than $73 billion in early 2018, also decided to tackle education reform.[4] He is an advocate of charter schools. In 2015, he gave $100 million to the public school system of Newark, New Jersey, a city with a poverty rate of almost 30 percent in 2016.[5] The understanding was that the city would spend some of that money on charter schools.

While some evidence suggests Newark students have improved their reading since 2015, much of Zuckerberg's money went to consultants and misguided attempts to get rid of

Teacher Shanel Sommers looks over the work of one of her third graders at KIPP Thrive Academy in September 2015. The new school is in what had been the closed Eighteenth Avenue School in Newark, New Jersey.

teachers whose contracts were protected by law. Zuckerberg is planning to expand his charter school efforts to California. Some observers believe his money could help create more high-quality schools. Others, however, bring up familiar criticisms of charter schools. They point out that, because charter schools have more power to expel troubled students or exclude students with disabilities, a growth in charter schools will not help all students in need.

Gates and Zuckerberg are not the only wealthy people involved in shaping education policy. Many hedge funds, or partnerships designed to help very wealthy people invest their money, put money into charter schools. On one hand, this money has the power to make big changes in the structure and availability of certain types of education, even if those changes are not always successful. On the other hand, wealthy philanthropists and investors like Gates and Zuckerberg are not accountable to the government or the public school system. Additionally, some critics worry that putting the power to make decisions about education policy in the hands of the wealthiest Americans means the culture and interests of low- and middle-income citizens are not and will not be represented.

INTERNATIONAL COMPETITION

The United States is among the wealthiest countries in the world, and its wealth gives it a great deal of power in political and economic affairs. The history of twentieth-century American education shows that many powerful people are eager to maintain that wealth. They want to do that by making sure the next generation of students is prepared to succeed in high-paying careers, especially in rapidly growing fields such as engineering, technology, and the internet.

In 2012, President Barack Obama's administration announced it would try to increase the number of college graduates in science, technology, engineering, and mathematics (STEM) fields by one million.[6] By February 2016, the administration had secured $1 billion in private funding for STEM education.[7] In addition, 350 colleges and universities agreed to recruit more underrepresented STEM students.[8] And a White House science fair raised awareness of STEM education.

The administration of President Donald Trump has continued the push to expand funding and increase attention for STEM programs. In September 2017, Trump signed a memo assigning $200 million of Department of Education funds to grants for STEM education for women and minorities.[9] Supporters say this will help the United States compete economically against

GIRLS WHO CODE

Girls Who Code is a nonprofit organization that tries to address the gender imbalance between men and women in STEM fields by teaching school-age girls coding and other science and engineering skills. The organization offers after-school and summer programs for girls in grades 6 through 12, and it hopes to reach 40,000 girls across the country.[10]

countries like China and India, which are increasing their numbers of STEM graduates. These cheerleaders for STEM programs in the United States see a direct connection between an increase or improvement in STEM education and the growth of the US economy. Critics of this narrow focus on STEM education say education should be about more than economic competition with other countries. They urge policymakers to value all parts of a child's education equally.

LYNDON B. JOHNSON'S WAR ON POVERTY

In 1964, President Lyndon B. Johnson announced his plan to wage war on poverty. Johnson was very interested in lessening income inequality in the United States. His war included laws to expand Social Security benefits, offer food stamps to people struggling to buy food, expand funding to poorer schools, and establish other programs to promote economic opportunity. These initiatives were successful in fighting poverty. A study from Columbia University found that between 1967 and 2012, poverty decreased from 26 percent to 16 percent.[11] Most of the laws Johnson introduced are still in place today.

US EDUCATION POLICY

There is an ongoing US education policy debate about the role the federal government should play in supervising schools and setting educational standards. For many years, the law known as No Child Left Behind was at the forefront of that debate. No Child Left Behind began in the 1960s as the Elementary and Secondary Education Act (ESEA). The goal of ESEA was to provide more national funding to schools with disadvantaged students, as part of President Lyndon B. Johnson's larger plan to address poverty. ESEA was updated many times over the years and became No Child Left Behind in 2002.

No Child Left Behind also tried to soothe American anxiety about education and the economy by creating new national tests for kids and punishing schools that did not meet certain standards. For example, schools that did not meet certain standards for "yearly progress," as defined by the state, would have to give away some of their funding to pay for tutoring or to give away "school choice," or voucher money.[12] Like ESEA, No Child Left Behind tried to increase the federal government's role in education. Some people criticized the law for punishing troubled schools by shutting them down or taking away some of their money, which sometimes left low-income students without a local school.

In 2015, a new law replaced No Child Left Behind. Every Student Succeeds Act (ESSA) keeps No Child Left Behind's testing standards but gets rid of punishments for low-performing schools. The law also gives more power over monitoring schools to the states. ESSA is also experimenting with weighted student funding, implementing the process in 50 districts. Under weighted student funding, districts spend the same amount of money on each student, with extra money given to students with special needs. The strategy combines elements of school choice with the push to reduce inequalities in spending on students.

President Barack Obama signed the "Every Student Succeeds Act" on December 10, 2015. The law intended to set US public schools on a new course of accountability.

ESSA took effect in the 2017–2018 school year. Critics of the law say giving state governments more power over public schools can leave students in poverty even more vulnerable because the testing mandates will not help close the achievement gap. Critics also say more federal money and attention are needed to fix these problems.

THE TRUMP ADMINISTRATION

Generally speaking, the Trump administration has embraced school choice, vouchers, and charter programs as part of its education policy. Trump's secretary of education, Betsy DeVos, is a controversial figure in the world of class and education. DeVos does not have a background in education, but she worked for many years as a public supporter of school choice in her home state of Michigan. DeVos is married to Dick DeVos, a billionaire whose family co-owns Amway, a health and beauty company. In Michigan, she donated millions of dollars to promote school choice initiatives and charter schools. The results were mixed. While a 2013 Stanford University study showed some gains made by children in Michigan charter schools, Michigan journalists point out that the charter system has decreased the racial and socioeconomic diversity of schools. Michigan still tends to perform poorly on national assessments of student math and reading. Supporters of school choice are excited by DeVos's appointment. Others fear she will support cuts to public school funding.

Before her confirmation hearing in January 2017, DeVos explained her philosophy of education:

> Parents no longer believe that a one-size-fits-all model of learning meets the needs of every child, and they know other options exist, whether magnet, virtual, charter, home, religious, or any combination thereof. . . . I am a firm believer that parents should be empowered to choose the learning environment that's best for their individual children.[13]

Despite DeVos's stated preference for school choice and past advocacy for charter systems, most money for US schools still comes from state and local funds, and the vast majority of children still attend traditional public schools. It is unclear whether DeVos will persuade her colleagues and the public to move policy further in the direction of school choice.

THE FUTURE OF CLASS AND EDUCATION

If current trends continue, class differences in the United States will become larger over time. If the current structures of the education system stay as they are, unevenly funded public schools, exclusive private schools, and frustrated teachers and families will remain the reality. The story of class and education in America is one about the thrill of imagining ideals—of equal opportunity to learn, of brave repairs to old injustices, of education as the key to success. It is also the story of the hard, often slow work of rethinking the systems and ideas that have brought the country to this point.

Horace Mann's words, "Education . . . is a great equalizer of the conditions of men," express a hope more than a reality.[16] To make his words true, the next generation of learners will have to use their education to rethink an old problem: how to equalize Americans once and for all.

DISCUSSION STARTERS

- If you had billions of dollars to spend on America's education system, what would you spend it on, and why?

- Do you agree with those who argue that educating more scientists and mathematicians will improve the economy? Why or why not?

- Imagine you are at a policy meeting at the US Department of Education. Make your argument either for or against giving vouchers to more public school students.

ESSENTIAL FACTS

SIGNIFICANT EVENTS

- Massachusetts had public schools as early as the 1600s and required everyone to learn how to read.

- By the early 1800s, many states began moving toward free mandatory education for all citizens. But educating enslaved people was illegal. The end of slavery brought a wave of new schools and colleges for newly freed African Americans.

- The 1896 Supreme Court case *Plessy v. Ferguson* made racial segregation legal. The 1954 Supreme Court case *Brown v. Board of Education* made official racial segregation illegal in schools.

- In 1965, Lyndon B. Johnson helped pass the Elementary and Secondary Education Act (ESEA) as part of his plan to fight poverty. The law gave more federal money and supervision to low-income schools.

- In 2002, ESEA was renamed No Child Left Behind, a controversial law that increased federal power over public schools and included plans to shut down or take money away from poorly performing schools.

- In 2015, Every Student Succeeds Act became law, keeping No Child Left Behind's testing standards and getting rid of punishments for low-performing schools.

- In 2017, New York and California created programs offering different amounts of free college tuition.

- The 2018 report "Healing Our Divided Society: Investing in America Fifty Years after the Kerner Report" showed that racial inequality in the United States' educational system still exists.

KEY PLAYERS

- Horace Mann was one of the first advocates for universal public education in the United States.

- Booker T. Washington founded the Tuskegee Institute and encouraged education as a key to comfortable class status for African Americans.

- The Black Panthers provided free breakfasts to 20,000 children across the country so they could focus on learning instead of hunger.

- Michelle Rhee used controversial methods as head of the Washington, DC, public school system from 2007 to 2010.

- Bill Gates invested hundreds of millions of dollars in the Common Core State Standards.

- Mark Zuckerberg gave $100 million to the public school system of Newark, New Jersey.

- NYC Men Teach works to hire male teachers of color to provide role models to the 43 percent of students in New York City public school classrooms who are nonwhite males.

IMPACT ON SOCIETY

At all levels of education, from preschool to university, a student's socioeconomic class affects the individual's experience in school and likelihood of succeeding academically. The United States has a nationwide public school system, and all children have the right to attend school for free. However, inequalities in school funding mean students in different parts of the country and in different areas of a city have very different school experiences. In addition, although many people think education is a tool for achieving wealth and status, research shows that class inequality can cancel out some of the benefits of education. Even with the same educational opportunities, people of different classes face different obstacles to wealth and success.

QUOTE

"Education . . . is a great equalizer of the conditions of men."

—*Horace Mann, education reformer in the 1800s*

GLOSSARY

ACHIEVEMENT GAP
Any significant and persistent difference in academic performance or educational attainment between different groups of students by race, ethnicity, or economic status.

AFFIRMATIVE ACTION
The practice of giving admissions preference to students from groups that have traditionally been discriminated against, such as females and racial minorities.

CHARTER SCHOOL
A public school that is partly funded by private money, such as from donors, and that can set many of its own rules.

CURRICULUM
The plan or course of study in a school; a plan for what lessons and information will be taught and how students will learn them.

DISTRICT
A geographical area decided on by a national, state, or local government; a public school district is an area served by public schools and supervised by the officials of that district.

EDUCATION POLICY
The decisions national, state, and local governments make about education, including funding, curricula, hiring of and standards for teachers, and special programs.

GRANT
A gift of money intended for a certain purpose, such as college tuition.

INCOME
Money received from work or investments.

MAGNET SCHOOL
A type of public school that accepts students from a wide geographical area and usually has special programs or areas of study, such as science or performing arts.

PRIVATE SCHOOL
A school that does not take government money and does not have to obey all the government's rules for public education; it is not required to admit all students and usually charges tuition for a student to attend.

PUBLIC SCHOOL
A school funded with money from local, state, and national governments and run according to government rules; students do not have to pay tuition and are guaranteed admission.

SCHOLARSHIP
A gift of money for a student's school tuition or school supplies.

SOCIOECONOMIC CLASS
A group of people who make a similar amount of money and share some aspects of their lifestyles as a result; *socioeconomic status* is another term for socioeconomic class.

UNION
An organized association of workers, often in a trade or profession, formed to protect and further their rights and interests.

VOUCHER
Government money given directly to a student or family instead of being used as part of a public school budget; children can use vouchers to pay part or all of their tuition at a private school.

ADDITIONAL
RESOURCES

SELECTED BIBLIOGRAPHY

Goldrick-Rab, Sara. *Paying the Price: College Costs, Financial Aid, and the Betrayal of the American Dream*. Chicago, IL: U of Chicago P, 2016. Print.

Goldstein, Dana. *The Teacher Wars: A History of America's Most Embattled Profession*. New York: Anchor, 2015. Print.

Lareau, Annette. *Unequal Childhoods: Class, Race, and Family Life*. Berkeley, CA: U of California P, 2011. Print.

Neem, Johann N. *Democracy's Schools: The Rise of Public Education in America*. Baltimore, MD: Johns Hopkins UP, 2017. Print.

FURTHER READINGS

Eboch, M. M. *Race and Economics*. Minneapolis: Abdo, 2018. Print.

Harris, Duchess, and Rebecca Rowell. *The American Middle Class*. Minneapolis: Abdo, 2019. Print.

Tonatiuh, Duncan, and Adriana Sananes. *Separate Is Never Equal: Sylvia Mendez and Her Family's Fight for Desegregation*. New York: Abrams, 2014.

ONLINE RESOURCES

To learn more about class and education, visit **abdobooklinks.com**. These links are routinely monitored and updated to provide the most current information available.

MORE INFORMATION

For more information on this subject, contact or visit the following organizations:

CLASS ACTION
30 Germania Street
Building L
Jamaica Plain, MA 02130
617-477-8635
classism.org

Class Action is a nonprofit organization that works to end classism in the United States. It offers workshops, educational courses, and consulting services that address issues of class inequality.

NATIONAL CENTER FOR EDUCATION RESEARCH
Institute of Education Sciences
550 Twelfth Street SW
Washington, DC 20202
202-245-6940
ies.ed.gov/ncer

The National Center for Education Research, which is run by the US Department of Education, researches trends and issues in education in the United States.

NATIONAL EDUCATION POLICY CENTER
School of Education
University of Colorado, Boulder
Boulder, CO 80309-0249
802-383-0058
nepc.colorado.edu

The National Education Policy Center conducts and publishes research on education policy in the United States.

SOURCE NOTES

CHAPTER 1. PRE-K FOR ALL

1. Dana Goldstein. "Bill De Blasio's Pre-K Crusade." *Atlantic*. Atlantic Media Company, 7 Sept. 2016. Web. 11 Apr. 2018.

2. "Explorers Academy Preschool." *Brooklyn Explorers Academy*. Brooklyn Explorers Academy, n.d. Web. 11 Apr. 2018.

3. Amy Zimmer. "Want a Free Pre-K Seat at a Private School? Start Looking When Your Kid's 2." *DNA Info*. New York Public Radio, 29 Jan. 2016. Web. 11 Apr. 2018.

4. "Pre-K for All Handbook 2016–17 for District Schools and Pre-K Centers." *NYC Department of Education*. New York City Department of Education, 2018. Web. 11 Apr. 2018.

5. Eric Westervelt. "The Research Argument for NYC's Preschool Plan for 3-Year-Olds." *NPR*. NPR, 25 Apr. 2017. Web. 11 Apr. 2018.

6. Kate Taylor. "Is '3-K for All' Good for All? De Blasio's Preschool Plan Troubles Some." *New York Times*. New York Times, 10 May 2017. Web. 11 Apr. 2018.

7. "America's Shrinking Middle Class: A Close Look at Changes within Metropolitan Areas." *Pew Research Center*. Pew Research Center, 11 May 2016. Web. 11 Apr. 2018.

8. Casey Burgat and Charles Hunt. "How Wealthy Are Our Representatives?" LegBranch.com. Legislative Branch Capacity Working Group, 3 Oct. 2017. Web. 11 Apr. 2018.

CHAPTER 2. HISTORY OF CLASS AND EDUCATION

1. Charla Bear. "American Indian Boarding Schools Haunt Many." *NPR*. NPR, 12 May 2008. Web. 11 Apr. 2018.

2. David Rhode, Kristina Cooke, and Himanshu-Ojha. "The Decline of the 'Great Equalizer.'" *Atlantic*. Atlantic Media Company, 19 Dec. 2012. Web. 11 Apr. 2018.

3. Daphne Martschenko. "IQ Tests Have a Dark, Controversial History—but They're Finally Being Used for Good." *Business Insider*. Business Insider, 11 Oct. 2017. Web. 11 Apr. 2018.

CHAPTER 3. STRUCTURES OF CLASS AND EDUCATION

1. Laura Shin. "The Racial Wealth Gap: Why A Typical White Household Has 16 Times the Wealth of a Black One." *Forbes*. Forbes Media, 25 Jan. 2016. Web. 11 Apr. 2018.

2. Abigail Bessler. "A Black College Student Has the Same Chances of Getting a Job as a White High School Dropout." *ThinkProgress*. ThinkProgress, 24 June 2014. Web. 11 Apr. 2018.

3. Andrea King Collier. "The Black Panthers: Revolutionaries, Free Breakfast Pioneers." *Plate*. National Geographic, 4 Nov. 2015. Web. 11 Apr. 2018.

4. Bessler, "A Black College Student."

5. Robert L. Osgood. *The History of Special Education: A Struggle for Equality in American Public Schools*. Westport, CT: Praeger, 2008. Print. 32–33.

6. Carol J. Carter. "Why Aren't Low-Income Students Succeeding in School?" *HuffPost*. Oath, 19 Mar. 2013. Web. 11 Apr. 2018.

CHAPTER 4. CLASS AND THE PUBLIC SCHOOL SYSTEM

1. "Fast Facts: Back to School Statistics." *National Center for Education Statistics*. US Department of Education, 2018. Web. 11 Apr. 2018.

2. Jack Jennings. "Proportion of US Students in Private Schools Is 10 Percent and Declining." *HuffPost*. Oath, 28 Mar. 2013. Web. 11 Apr. 2018.

3. "Public School Revenue Sources." *National Center for Education Statistics*. US Department of Education, Mar. 2018. Web. 11 Apr. 2018.

4. Cory Turner, et al. "Why America's Schools Have a Money Problem." *NPR*. NPR, 18 Apr. 2016. Web. 11 Apr. 2018.

5. Elizabeth A. Harris and Kristin Hussey. "In Connecticut, a Wealth Gap Divides Neighboring Schools." *New York Times*. New York Times, 11 Sept. 2016. Web. 11 Apr. 2018.

6. "Teacher and Principal School Report: Methodology." *Scholastic*. Scholastic, 2018. Web. 11 Apr. 2018.

7. "Teacher and Principal School Report: Educators' Funding: Priorities and Personal Spending." *Scholastic*. Scholastic, 2018. Web. 11 Apr. 2018.

8. Harris and Hussey, "In Connecticut, a Wealth Gap."

9. Harris and Hussey, "In Connecticut, a Wealth Gap."

10. Rick Green. "State Faces Big Task Complying with Judge's Ruling." *Hartford Courant*. Hartford Courant, 7 Sept. 2016. Web. 9 Apr. 2018.

11. Jacqueline Rabe Thomas. "Court to Hear School Funding Case amid Discord over Education Aid." *CT Mirror*. Connecticut News Project, 28 Sept. 2017. Web. 11 Apr. 2018.

12. Anya Kamenetz. "When Integrating a School, Does It Matter If You Use Class Instead of Race?" *NPR*. NPR, 29 Feb. 2016. Web. 11 Apr. 2018.

13. Alia Wong. "The Activity Gap." *Atlantic*. Atlantic Media Company, 30 Jan. 2015. Web. 11 Apr. 2018.

14. Chris Weller. "Chance the Rapper Is on a Mission to Prove That Public Schools Still Matter." *Business Insider*. Business Insider, 7 Sept. 2017. Web. 11 Apr. 2018.

15. "The National School Lunch Program." *US Department of Agriculture Food and Nutrition Service*. US Department of Agriculture, Nov. 2017. Web. 11 Apr. 2018.

16. Anthony Lonetree. "Shaming over School Lunch Debts Has to Stop, Minnesota Legislator Says." *StarTribune*. StarTribune, 21 Nov. 2017. Web. 18 Feb. 2018.

17. Lonetree, "Shaming over School Lunch."

18. Bettina Elias Siegel. "Shaming Children So Parents Will Pay the School Lunch Bill." *New York Times*. New York Times, 30 Apr. 2017. Web. 11 Apr. 2018.

CHAPTER 5. PRIVATE SCHOOLS AND HOMESCHOOLING

1. "Fast Facts." *National Center for Education Statistics*. US Department of Education, 2018. Web. 11 Apr. 2018.

2. "Statistics about Non-Public Education in the United States." *US Department of Education, Office of Innovation and Improvement*. US Department of Education, 2 Dec. 2016. Web. 11 Apr. 2018.

3. "Tuition and Financial Aid." *Phillips Academy Andover*. Phillips Academy Andover, n.d. Web. 11 Apr. 2018.

4. "Tuition and Financial Aid."

5. Meg P. Bernhard. "The Making of a Harvard Feeder School." *Harvard Crimson*. Harvard Crimson, 13 Dec. 2013. Web. 11 Apr. 2018.

6. Jenny Anderson. "For Minority Students at Elite New York Private Schools, Admittance Doesn't Bring Acceptance." *New York Times*. New York Times, 19 Oct. 2012. Web. 11 Apr. 2018.

7. "Tuition and Enrollment." *Kumon of Piscataway [NJ]*. Kumon, n.d. Web. 11 Apr. 2018.

8. Robert Frank. "Meet the $1,250-an-Hour Tutor." *CNBC*. CNBC, 12 Dec. 2013. Web. 18 Feb. 2018.

9. Frank, "Meet the $1,250-an-Hour Tutor."

10. "Statistics about Non-Public Education."

11. "Schools and Tuition." *NCEA*. National Catholic Education Association, 2018. Web. 11 Apr. 2018.

12. "Catholic School Fact Sheet." *United States Conference of Catholic Bishops*. United States Conference of Catholic Bishops, 2018. Web. 11 Apr. 2018.

13. Jessica Huseman. "Homeschooling Regulations by State." *ProPublica*. Pro Publica, 27 Aug. 2015. Web. 11 Apr. 2018.

SOURCE NOTES
CONTINUED

CHAPTER 6. STRATEGIES FOR CHANGING US SCHOOLING

1. "Fast Facts: Charter Schools." *National Center for Education Statistics*. US Department of Education, 2018. Web. 11 Apr. 2018.

2. Alia Wong. "The Most Polarizing Education Reformer in New York City." *Atlantic*. Atlantic Media Company, 22 Sept. 2017. Web. 11 Apr. 2018.

3. Sarah Carr. "How Strict Is Too Strict?" *Atlantic*. Atlantic Media Company, 17 Nov. 2014. Web. 11 Apr. 2108.

4. "How Is KIPP Structured?" *KIPP*. Kipp Foundation, n.d. Web. 11 Apr. 2018.

5. George Joseph. "Where Charter-School Suspensions Are Concentrated." *Atlantic*. Atlantic Media Company, 16 Sept. 2016. Web. 11 Apr. 2018.

6. Kevin Hart. "Study: Charter Schools Not Keeping Their Promise to America's Students." *National Education Association*. National Education Association, 2017. Web. 11 Apr. 2018.

7. Marcy Crouch. "Magnet Schools and Other Means of Desegregation." *Ethics of Development in a Global Environment*. Stanford University, 26 July 1999. Web. 11 Apr. 2018.

8. "History of Magnets." *Magnet Schools of America*. Magnet Schools of America, 2017. Web. 11 Apr. 2018.

CHAPTER 7. CLASS AND TEACHING

1. "Fast Facts: Teacher Trends." *National Center for Education Statistics*. US Department of Education, 2018. Web. 11 Apr. 2018.

2. "Table 11.60. Estimated Average Annual Salary of Teachers in Public Elementary and Secondary Schools, by State: Selected Years, 1969–70 through 2012–13." *National Center for Education Statistics*. US Department of Education, 2013. Web. 11 Apr. 2018.

3. "Fast Facts: Teacher Trends."

4. "The State of Racial Diversity in the Educator Workforce." *US Department of Education*. US Department of Education, July 2016. Web. 11 Apr. 2018.

5. Patrick Wall. "How to Get More Men of Color Teaching in the Classroom." *Atlantic*. Atlantic Media Company, 21 June 2016. Web. 11 Apr. 2018.

6. Sara Mead. "The Capital of Education Reform." *US News & World Report*. US News & World Report, 20 Apr. 2017. Web. 11 Apr. 2018.

7. Dana Goldstein. *The Teacher Wars: A History of America's Most Embattled Profession*. New York: Anchor, 2015. Print. 79.

CHAPTER 8. CLASS AND HIGHER EDUCATION

1. *Studentmarch.org*. Student March, n.d. Web. 11 Apr. 2018.

2. Kaitlin Mulhere. "The Million Student March Protestors Say They're Just Getting Started." *Time*. Time, 13 Nov. 2015. Web. 11 Apr. 2018.

3. "Fast Facts: Enrollment." *National Center for Education Statistics*. US Department of Education, 2018. Web. 11 Apr. 2018.

4. "Immediate College Enrollment Rate." *National Center for Education Statistics*. US Department of Education, Jan. 2018. Web. 11 Apr. 2018.

5. Jia Tolentino. "All the Greedy Young Abigail Fishers and Me." *Jezebel*. Gizmodo Media Group, 28 June 2016. Web. 11 Apr. 2018.

6. "Fast Facts: Tuition Costs of Colleges and Universities." *National Center for Education Statistics*. US Department of Education, 2018. Web. 11 Apr. 2018.

7. Jon O'Donnell. "Your 2017–2018 Pell Grant Guide: What You Need to Know about Eligibility, Limits, and Deadlines." *Nitro College*. Nitro College, 5 July 2017. Web. 11 Apr. 2018.

8. "Tuition-Free Degree Program: The Excelsior Scholarship." *New York State*. New York State, n.d. Web. 11 Apr. 2018.

9. Elena Holodny. "How Much Student Loan Debt People Owe in Each State Shows Some Graduates Are Getting Screwed." *Business Insider*. Business Insider, 17 Nov. 2017. Web. 11 Apr. 2018.

10. Dave Berry. "Legacy Applicants Have Admissions Advantage." *College Confidential*. College Confidential, 2018. Web. 11 Apr. 2018.

CHAPTER 9. LOOKING AHEAD

1. "Bill Gates." *Forbes*. Forbes Media, 11 Apr. 2018. Web. 11 Apr. 2018.

2. *Bill & Melinda Gates Foundation*. Bill & Melinda Gates Foundation, 2018. Web. 11 Apr. 2018.

3. "Foundation Fact Sheet." *Bill & Melinda Gates Foundation*. Bill & Melinda Gates Foundation, 2018. Web. 11 Apr. 2018.

4. "Mark Zuckerberg." *Forbes*. Forbes Media, 11 Apr. 2018. Web. 11 Apr. 2018.

5. "Quickfacts: Newark City, New Jersey." *US Census Bureau*. US Department of Commerce, n.d. Web. 11 Apr. 2018.

6. "Energy 101 Dialogue." *Office of Energy Efficiency and Renewable Energy*. US Department of Energy, n.d. Web. 11 Apr. 2018.

7. Jo Handelsman and Megan Smith. "STEM for All." *White House: President Barack Obama*. White House Archives, 11 Feb. 2016. Web. 23 Apr. 2018.

8. Handelsman and Smith, "STEM for All."

9. "President Trump Signs Memorandum for STEM Education Funding." *White House*. White House, 26 Sept. 2017. Web. 11 Apr. 2018.

10. "About Us." *Girls Who Code*. Girls Who Code, 2018. Web. 11 Apr. 2018.

11. Dylan Matthews. "Everything You Need to Know about the War on Poverty." *Washington Post*. Washington Post, 8 Jan. 2014. Web. 11 Apr. 2018.

12. Alyson Klein. "No Child Left Behind Overview: Definitions, Requirements, Criticisms, and More." *Education Week*. Editorial Projects in Education, 10 Apr. 2015. Web. 11 Apr. 2018.

13. Ed Kilgore. "Does Betsy DeVos Really Believe in Public Schools?" *New York*. New York Media, 18 Jan. 2017. Web. 11 Apr. 2018.

14. Russell Contreras. "Study: US Inequality Persists 50 Years after Landmark Report." *ABC News*. ABC News, 27 Feb. 2018. Web. 4 Mar. 2018.

15. Contreras, "Study: US Inequality Persists."

16. David Rhode, Kristina Cooke, and Himanshu-Ojha. "The Decline of the 'Great Equalizer.'" *Atlantic*. Atlantic Monthly Group, 19 Dec. 2012. Web. 11 Apr. 2018.

INDEX

ABOUT THE
AUTHORS

DUCHESS HARRIS, JD, PHD

Professor Harris is the chair of the American Studies department at Macalester College and curator of the Duchess Harris Collection of ABDO books. She is the author and coauthor of recently released ABDO books including *Hidden Human Computers: The Black Women of NASA*, *Black Lives Matter*, and *Race and Policing*.

Before working with ABDO, she authored several other books on the topics of race, culture, and American history. She served as an associate editor for *Litigation News*, the American Bar Association Section of Litigation's quarterly flagship publication, and was the first editor in chief of *Law Raza*, an interactive online journal covering race and the law, published at William Mitchell College of Law. She has earned a PhD in American Studies from the University of Minnesota and a JD from William Mitchell College of Law.

A. W. BUCKEY

A. W. Buckey is a writer and tutor living in Brooklyn, New York City.